Comprehension Success 1

James Driver

Preface

Comprehension is a comprehensive activity that involves many different aspects of English. This book uses the traditional role of comprehension – asking questions on the content of short texts – as a starting-point from which to investigate, in depth, a variety of different kinds of writing.

The thirty double-pages of comprehensions offer a wide variety of texts – examples from information books, action rhymes, realia such as postcards and notices, children's fiction, fable, catalogues, comic strips, picture books, poems and legends – a whole range of genres, drawn from authentic texts.

The pupils are then encouraged to use a range of strategies to discover meaning. They will practise locating, selecting, collating, identifying, using, retrieving, examining and re-presenting ideas and information, and, by employing quotation, deduction and inference, find that their confidence as readers who fully appreciate a text will continue to grow.

There are three sections on most of the question pages. Section A contains the most straightforward recall questions. The questions in Section B often call for a deeper insight into the nature of the text. The knowledge gained from answering one, or both, of these two sets of questions is used in Section C, which offers a prompt for a creative writing activity, in the same genre as the selected text.

The confidence that comes from being able to understand the main points about the facts, characters and events that appear in a broad range of texts encourages readers to read more widely and enables them to gain a better understanding of how writing, its form, language and content, works. This, in turn, should lead to a faster development of their ability as writers.

OXFORD
UNIVERSITY PRESS

Great Clarendon Street, Oxford OX2 6DP

Oxford University Press is a department of the University of Oxford.
It furthers the University's objective of excellence in research, scholarship, and education by publishing worldwide in

Oxford New York

Auckland Cape Town Dar es Salaam Hong Kong Karachi
Kuala Lumpur Madrid Melbourne Mexico City Nairobi
New Delhi Shanghai Taipei Toronto

With offices in

Argentina Austria Brazil Chile Czech Republic France Greece
Guatemala Hungary Italy Japan Poland Portugal Singapore
South Korea Switzerland Thailand Turkey Ukraine Vietnam

Oxford is a registered trade mark of Oxford University Press in the UK and in certain other countries

© Oxford University Press 1998
First published 1998

20 19

ISBN: 978-0-19-834178-9

Typeset and designed by Oxford Designers & Illustrators, Oxford

Printed in Singapore by KHL Printing Co Pte Ltd

Paper used in the production of this book is a natural, recyclable product made from wood grown in sustainable forests. The manufacturing process conforms to the environmental regulations of the country of origin.

Contents

Elephants	Information book	4
Hedgehogs	Magazine page	6
Incey Wincey Spider	Action rhyme	8
Old Mother Hubbard	Nursery rhyme	10
A night-time adventure	Picture story	12
Billy and Belle	Picture story	14
Looking after a rabbit	Instructions	16
Bat boxes	Information book	18
Holiday postcards	Postcards	20
Nature diary	Diary	22
A cat always lands on its feet	Information book	24
Bones	Information book	26
Air pollution	Information book	28
The Wully-Wully	Children's story	30
Monsters	Children's story	32
The school skeleton	Children's story	34
Stickers	Catalogue	36
Fire Orders	Notice	38
Ancient Greece	Information book	40
Places	Information book	42
The Beano	Comic strip	44
Tintin	Comic strip	46
Fairy Story	Poem	48
The Alien and Mystery Creatures	Poems	50
The wind and the sun	Fable	52
Morgiana and Ali Baba	Legend	54
Art and the human body	Information book	56
Faces and masks	Information book	58
Life in an Indian village	Picture sequence	60
How to make a flick book	Instructions	62

Elephants

These pictures are from an information book on living things.

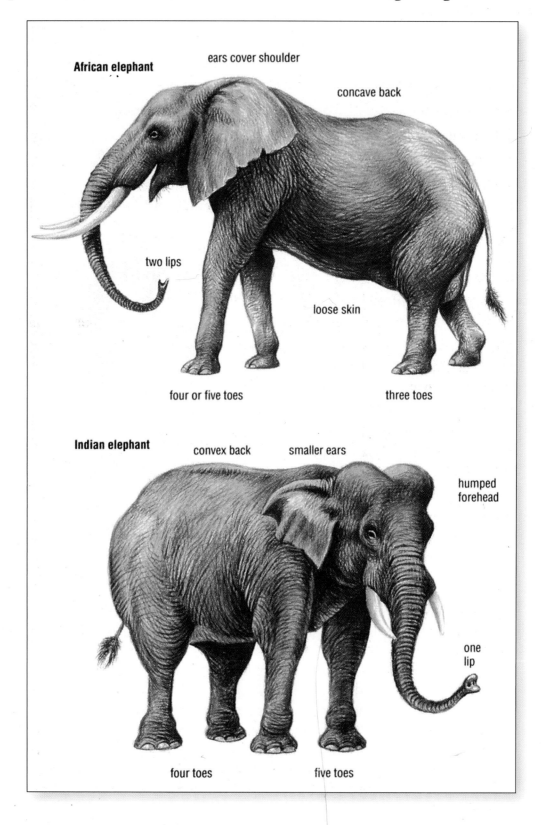

African elephant

ears cover shoulder

concave back

two lips

loose skin

four or five toes

three toes

Indian elephant

convex back

smaller ears

humped
forehead

one
lip

four toes

five toes

There are **two** kinds of elephant. The pictures and the words on the opposite page tell you how they are different.

1 Write down the name of **one** kind of elephant.

2 Write down the name of the **other** kind of elephant.

3 Which kind of elephant has smaller ears?

4 Which kind of elephant has a bumpy forehead?

5 Which kind of elephant has **three** toes on its back feet?

1 **a)** Do you think it would be more comfortable to ride on the back of an Indian elephant or an African elephant?

   b) Why do you think the elephant you chose would be more comfortable?

2 Imagine you find an elephant's foot print.
It is a footprint of a **front** foot.
It has **four** toes.
What sort of elephant made that footprint?

3 Imagine you find an elephant's foot print.
It is a footprint of a **back** foot.
It has **four** toes.
What sort of elephant made that footprint?

4 What do you think the word **concave** means?

Now show an animal you know well in the same way. Either draw the animal or cut out a picture, and write **labels** round the edge giving **information** about the animal.

Hedgehogs

This page comes from a children's comic, which has lots of facts about animals.

1 Hedgehogs live in piles of leaves, in hollow trees or underneath hedges.

2 When hedgehogs are scared they curl up into a prickly ball to protect themselves.

3 They are good swimmers and good climbers too, but they like to spend most of their time on the ground.

4 When they go looking for food at night, they sometimes walk for over two miles on their tiny legs!

A

1 Write down **one** place where hedgehogs live.
2 What do hedgehogs have covering their backs?
3 How do hedgehogs protect themselves when they are scared?
4 When do hedgehogs go out hunting for food?
5 Find a word in section 2 that means **defend**.

B

1 When do you think a hedgehog might need to swim?
2 When do you think a hedgehog might need to climb?
3 Why do you think hedgehogs like living in piles of leaves?
4 Write down the words that tell you hedgehogs are very fit.
5 What other facts about hedgehogs that **don't** appear here would
   you like to know? Think of **three** more things you would like to know about
   hedgehogs.

C

Write 4 paragraphs of **information** on an animal you know about.
You could take the elephant from the last page, and turn the labels into
longer sentences.

Incey Wincey Spider

This is an action rhyme to play with young children.

Incey Wincey spider
Climbing up the spout;

Down came the rain
And washed the spider out;

Out came the sun
And dried up all the rain;

Incey Wincey spider
Climbing up again.

1 Where is the spider trying to go?

2 What stops the spider from getting where it wants to go?

3 What helps the spider to carry on with its journey?

4 Write down the word used in the rhyme that tells us what the spider is doing in the first picture.

5 The rhyme says "Out came the sun". Look at the pictures. Where had the sun been before it came out?

6 Write down the word used in the rhyme that sounds the same as **spout**.

1 In the first picture the spider is **inside**; why is the spider shown **outside** in the second picture?

2 If the spider was **inside**, explain how it was affected by the rain.

3 a) Think of a word that could take the place of **climbing**.
   b) Think of a word that could take the place of **washed**.

This rhyme is often played as part of a game with little children. You can invent actions to suit the words.

1 You have been asked to write an **instruction book** telling how to play the game. Copy out the first two lines. Then write down the actions you think the children should do whenever they mention Incey Wincey spider. (Should they wriggle their fingers? Should they run around with their hands on the floor?)

2 Copy out the second set of lines. Write underneath how to show with your hands that the rain was coming down.

3 Copy out the third set of lines. Write underneath how to show with your hands that the sun had come out.

Old Mother Hubbard

This is part of an old nursery rhyme which has been known for over two hundred years.

She went to the tailor's
　To buy him a coat;
When she came back
　He was riding a goat.

She went to the hatter's
　To buy him a hat;
When she came back
　He was feeding her cat.

She went to the barber's
　To buy him a wig;
When she came back
　He was dancing a jig.

She went to the cobbler's
　To buy him some shoes;
When she came back
　He was reading the news.

Old Mother Hubbard and her Dog is quite a long rhyme. In each verse the dog does more and more extraordinary things.

1 Why does Mother Hubbard go to the tailor's?

2 Why was Mother Hubbard surprised when she came back from the tailor?

3 How was the Dog helpful when Mother Hubbard went to the hatter's?

4 What was stuck in the Dog's hat?

5 What did Mother Hubbard buy at the barber's?

6 What does a cobbler sell?

7 Make a list of all the animals that appear in the pictures.

1 When he had his hat on, what did the Dog do to show he was happy?

2 a) What do you think was the most amazing thing the Dog did?
b) Why do you think this was the most amazing thing he did?

3 a) If you were Old Mother Hubbard, what would you buy the Dog next?
b) Why would you choose this particular thing for the Dog?

4 Describe how these old illustrations are different from pictures in books today.

1 Here are two more verses about Old Mother Hubbard. Some of the words are missing. Copy the verses out filling in the gaps so that they make sense, and rhyme.

She went to the Baker's

To buy him a c _ _ _ ,

When she came back

He was swimming the l _ _ _ .

She went to the B _ _ _ _ _ _'s

To buy him some pork,

When she came back

He was taking a w _ _ _ .

2 Now try and write your own verse about Mother Hubbard and her Dog.

A night-time adventure

This is part of a picture story by Posy Simmonds, told through drawings and speech bubbles.

A

1 What sort of animal has the girl seen through the window?

2 Why does the animal look strange?

3 Why can't the little boy see this strange animal?

4 What do the children put on before they go downstairs?

5 What is the name of the cat?

6 What is the name of the cat's owner?

7 Why is the little boy surprised when he sees the cat?

B

1 a) What do you think is the little boy's favourite cuddly toy?
  b) How can you tell this is his favourite toy?

2 What does the girl **say** that shows you she wants the boy to be quiet?

3 What do the two children **do** so that they don't make a noise?

4 Why do you think the children are being so quiet?

5 Why can the little boy see out into the garden when he is downstairs?

6 Why is the cat cross?

7 Why does the writer put some of the words in **CAPITAL** letters?

C

This story starts one ordinary night, in an ordinary house, with two ordinary children. Then, suddenly, a very strange animal appears.

Write a **story** that starts one ordinary night, where you live, when a very unusual animal appears outside **your** window.

You might like the strange animal to be: a dog on roller skates
                                          a goldfish in a diving suit
                                          a horse on a bicycle

Try writing the speech between your characters, as here, or add some drawings.

13

Billy and Belle

This page from a picture story by Sarah Garland has some sentences of text, as well as the pictures and speech bubbles.

Mum and Dad were going to the hospital.

Billy and Belle were going to school with Mrs Plum, the school secretary.

A

1 a) Where are Mum and Dad going?
   b) How are Mum and Dad going to get there?

2 Why are they going there?

3 Where are Billy and Belle going?

4 a) What is the name of the woman who is taking Billy and Belle there?
   b) What job does she do?

B

Look carefully at the pictures. Look at what the different people are doing. Notice what the different people say to each other.

1 How can you tell that Mum will miss Belle?

2 How can you tell that Mum will be away from home for some time?

3 How can you tell that Dad is ready for a new baby in the house?

4 How can you tell that Billy is interested in the new baby?

5 How can you tell that Billy is a little bit worried about his mother?

C

1 Billy and Belle want the baby's name to begin with **B**, just like their names. Help them by making a **list** of three names for girls and three names for boys.

2 To welcome the new baby when their Mum comes back from the hospital Billy and Belle decide to make a **card**.

   Help them by drawing the card, and writing the message inside.

3 New babies sleep far more than older children. Mum and Dad decide to make a **notice** to pin on the baby's bedroom door.

   Help them by designing the notice, with the right words of warning.

Looking after a rabbit

This information book has funny pictures, to help you enjoy reading it.

How to Feed Your Rabbit

Whee! Plastic dishes make excellent Frisbees.

Make sure your rabbit's food bowl is too heavy for her to tip over. Do not use a plastic bowl. Your pet might gnaw it and hurt herself on the broken pieces.

Mmm! I just love water.

A drip-fed water bottle with a stainless steel spout is the safest and cleanest way of giving your pet fresh water.

Anyone for stick?

Keep a small piece of wood in the hutch for your rabbit to gnaw on. This will stop her teeth growing too long.

A

1 What is the rabbit's bowl used for?

2 What would happen if the rabbit's bowl was very light?

3 Why is it dangerous to give a rabbit a plastic bowl?

4 What should you use to give a rabbit its water?

5 Only **one** of these sentences is true. Write it down.
   a) Rabbits don't have front teeth.
   b) Rabbits' front teeth grow all the time.
   c) Rabbits' front teeth stay the same size.

6 Write down the word used on the opposite page that means a **rabbit's house**.

7 Write down the word used on the opposite page that means **chew**.

B

1 Why do you think the water bottle spout is made of a strong metal like stainless steel?

2 Why do you think you couldn't put the water in a bowl?

3 There are three pictures of cartoon rabbits on the opposite page.
   Two of the pictures show a rabbit doing things a real rabbit would do.
   One of the pictures shows a cartoon rabbit doing something silly.
   a) What is the rabbit doing in the silly picture?
   b) Why do you think the artist has done this drawing?

C

Imagine you are transported to a world where everything is back to front. In this world rabbits keep humans as pets!

Write a page of **instructions** that tells the rabbits **How to Feed Your Human**! Make your page look like the opposite page – use pictures as well as words.

Bat boxes

This page is from an information book on how to protect wildlife.

Nest boxes for small animals

Bats

Bats catch and eat a lot of insects at night. Most bats live in hollow trees and caves. There are not many hollow trees and caves now, and some bats live in old buildings.

Bat boxes

Some people help bats to find a home. They put up special boxes for the bats to live in. You can see two in the picture.

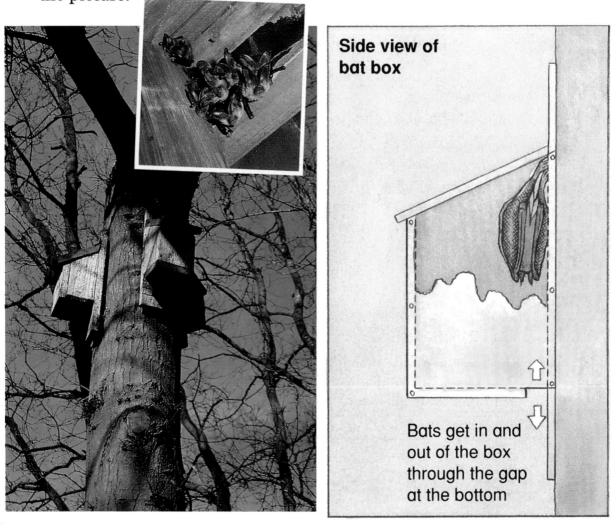

Side view of bat box

Bats get in and out of the box through the gap at the bottom

Bats are flying mammals. They sleep during the day and come out at night to search for food.

A

1 On the opposite page we are told what bats eat. What is this food?

2 Make a list of **four** different places where bats might make their homes.

3 Why does a bat box have a narrow gap in the floor?

4 At what time of the day would you expect to see a bat?

5 Write down a word in the piece of writing about bats that means **empty**.

6 **a)** Do bats live alone, or do bats live with other bats?
  b) How can you tell this from the pictures on the opposite page?

B

1 Why do you think the two bat boxes in the picture have been put so high up above the ground?

2 Why have people had to make boxes for bats to live in?

3 Some people are frightened by bats. Some people think they are useful. Would you like to have bats living near your home?

Explain why you would like, or hate, to have bats living near you.

C

One of the illustrations on the opposite page is a **diagram**.
A **diagram** is a drawing that shows how something is made or how something works. The **labels** on a diagram give information about the diagram. This **diagram** shows how a bat box is made and how the bat hangs upside down when it sleeps inside the bat box.

1 Copy the **diagram** from the opposite page.

Copy out these **labels** and draw lines from the **labels** so that they point to the right part of the **diagram**.

| sleeping bat | tree | sloping roof | front | side | entrance |

2 Draw a **diagram** and **label** it, of the room where you sleep.

Holiday postcards

These postcards were written by two children on holiday. They were writing to members of their family, about what they had done.

Monday
Dear Granny,
The sea is very warm! I went in as soon as we got here at six O'clock.
It took five hours! We got stuck on the motor way with hundreds of other cars. See you in three days.
Love
Sam

Mrs Ann Symmons,
Beach View,
Clifton,
Devon
EX3 7PR

Tuesday
Dear Aunty Jane,
Today I went fishing with my new rod. I didn't catch anything. I haven't been swimming yet but Sam has been everyday! It is far too cold for me. I am looking forward to tonight's supper – it's my favourite
Love John

Mrs Symmons,
13A, The Gove,
Patrickstown,
Tyne and Wear.
NC12 4AP

Wednesday
Dear Aunty Jane,
I went swimming yesterday and this morning. I saw some fish. I am going to try and catch them with John's fishing rod. We had chips last night.
Love
Sam

Jane Symmons,
13A, The Gove,
Patrickstown,
Tyne and Wear.

Thursday
Dear Uncle Clyde,
We have just got back from Granny's where Sam caught a fish in his net. It was too small to eat so I took it to the caravan to show Mum and Dad. Sam said we should take it to Granny's. Mum said we would spill it in the car
Love John.

Clyde Barker
48, Station Rd.,
Anserley,
West Midlands.
BW5 911

A

1 What are the names of the **two** children who are on holiday?

2 What kind of place have they gone to for their holiday?

3 How did they get there?

4 Why did it take them so long to get there?

5 What are they living in while they are on holiday?

6 How many **different** people do they send postcards to?

7 What does Sam use to catch the fish?

B

1 What do you think is Sam's favourite holiday activity?

2 What do you think John's hobby is?

3 How can you tell that the children's Granny lives by the sea?

4 What is John's favourite food?

5 What do you think the children were going to carry the fish in?

6 **a)** Who do you think wrote the **addresses** on the postcards?
   b) Explain why you have chosen this particular person.

C

Now write your own postcards. Choose a place you have been to, and write to one of your family about what you did there.

Nature diary

A diary is a record of what you have done or seen, day by day. This is a nature diary, for the month of June.

9th June. We went for a Nature Walk to-day. We were looking for different kinds of grass flowers. We found seven different kinds. We put them on the Nature Table.

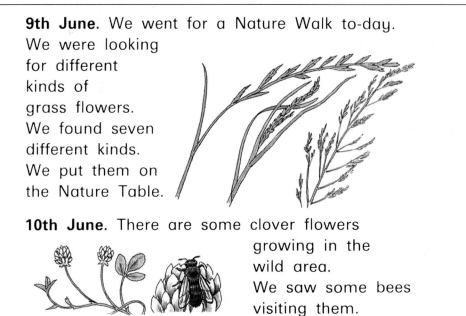

10th June. There are some clover flowers growing in the wild area. We saw some bees visiting them.

15th June. We found some cuckoo spit on the weeds in the wild area. It looks white and bubbly. It is made by insects called froghoppers. Baby froghoppers grow up inside the cuckoo spit.

22nd June. It is very warm to-day. At twelve o'clock the temperature was 23 degrees Centigrade. When we looked across the school field we could see the warm air rising from the ground. We saw a dragonfly over our pond.

A

1 What did the writer of the diary do on June 9th?

2 What was special about June 22nd?

3 Why did the bees like the wild area?

4 How can you tell this diary was kept by someone at a school?

5 Name **two** different plants mentioned in the diary that have flowers.

B

1 A cuckoo is a bird that strays into other birds' nests. Why do you think cuckoo spit is so-called?

2 Why do you think baby froghoppers live inside cuckoo spit?

3 What has the school made to encourage wildlife?

4 Would you like to go to the same school as the person who kept this diary? Explain why you think you would like, or dislike, that school.

C

The **diary** here tells you what happens on four different **days**.

Write a **diary** that covers the next five **minutes**!

Write down all the things that you do, all the things you see, the sounds that you hear and the thoughts that you have in the next five minutes!

Start like this:

Minute One: I have started on this task. I am feeling....

A cat always lands on its feet

This book is a mixture: the cat has a name, so it reads like a story; but the facts are shown in diagrams, so you know the writer wants to give you information.

Bella wants to find a tom cat.
She wants to mate and have kittens.
She goes to the park,
but a dog finds her first.
He runs at her, barking and snapping.
Bella arches her back and
tries to scratch the dog with her claws.
But the dog is not frightened.
He dances around Bella and teases her
while she hisses and spits at him.
How can she escape?
She sees a tree and
makes a dash for it.
She darts up the trunk,
gripping it with her claws.
The dog runs round and round
the tree and barks at Bella.
Bella stays up in the tree and
soon the dog goes home.

Bella is safe now.
She jumps down and
lands lightly on all four paws.

Even if Bella had fallen,
she would have landed on
her paws.
Cats twist in the air
when they fall.
They always land
the right way up.

A

1 Where does Bella think she will find a tom cat?

2 What finds Bella?

3 Write down the sound Bella makes when she is angry.

4 What part of her body does Bella use as a weapon?

5 Write down **two** words that are used on this page that begin with the letter **d** and tell us that Bella moved very quickly.

6 Why doesn't Bella slide down the tree trunk?

7 Why do you think the dog goes home?

B

1 Why is it safe for Bella to come down from the tree?

2 Why do cats always land on their feet?

C

Now describe the next incident of Bella the cat.

She is trying to catch the birds that sit on the roof. She crawls out of an upstairs window. She leaps up towards the roof. Her claws slip. She falls!

She is lucky that she is a cat. Cats always land on their feet.

Describe what it is like as she falls. Describe what she sees. As she twists through the air the sky, the roof, the windows, the garden below, all flash in front of her eyes. Is she scared? Or is it exciting? How does she feel?

Describe what it is like when she reaches the ground.

Is her heart thumping? Is she happy to be safe, or cross with the bird!

Bones

This information concentrates on pictures, with long captions.

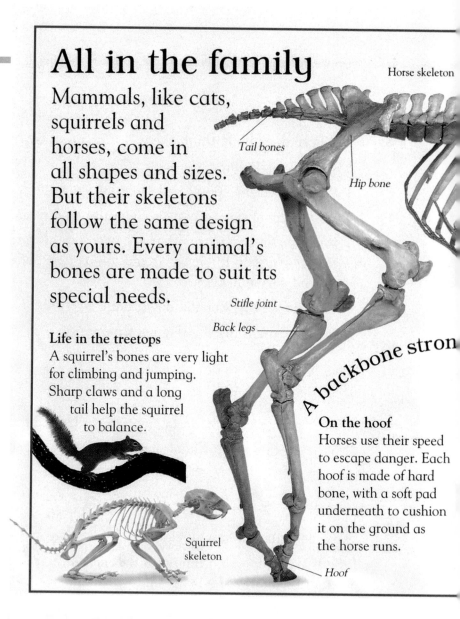

All in the family

Mammals, like cats, squirrels and horses, come in all shapes and sizes. But their skeletons follow the same design as yours. Every animal's bones are made to suit its special needs.

Horse skeleton

Tail bones

Hip bone

Stifle joint

Back legs

A backbone stron

Life in the treetops
A squirrel's bones are very light for climbing and jumping. Sharp claws and a long tail help the squirrel to balance.

On the hoof
Horses use their speed to escape danger. Each hoof is made of hard bone, with a soft pad underneath to cushion it on the ground as the horse runs.

Squirrel skeleton

Hoof

Different animals have bones of different shapes and sizes. They need different bones because they lead different lives.

1 How could you tell the skeleton of a horse from the skeleton of a cat?

2 What is the name for the main bone in an animal's head?

3 What is the name for an animal's backbone?

4 What does a squirrel use its tail for?

5 Find a word in the information about cats that means **bendy**.

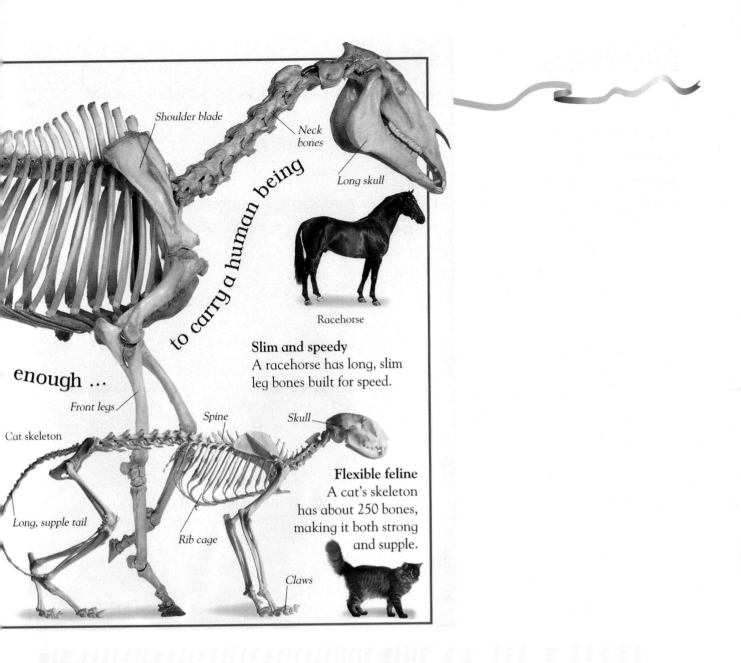

Shoulder blade

Neck bones

Long skull

to carry a human being

Racehorse

Slim and speedy
A racehorse has long, slim leg bones built for speed.

enough ...

Front legs

Spine

Skull

Cat skeleton

Flexible feline
A cat's skeleton has about 250 bones, making it both strong and supple.

Long, supple tail

Rib cage

Claws

B

1 Why does a racehorse have leg bones that are very long?

2 Why does a cat have so many bones?

3 Look at the skeleton of the cat. Why do you think the ribs are called a rib **cage**?

C

Your school buys an amazing **virtual reality machine**. It has a special programme that lets you try out the skeletons of other animals: **Horse, Squirrel, Cat**.

Write a Nature Diary, as on page 22, describing how one of these animals moves about.

Air pollution

This information book uses text, photos and diagrams to give you facts about the environment.

Causes of air pollution

Every day the air is made dirty by pollution. Most of this pollution is the waste gases and smoke which come from factories, and cars and lorries.

Breathing dirty air

Tiny hairs in our noses stop some of the larger pieces of dirt getting into our bodies. But they cannot stop the smoke and gases. These go into our lungs and may damage them. This can make us ill.

▲ Smoke from cigarettes gets into the lungs of smokers and non-smokers.

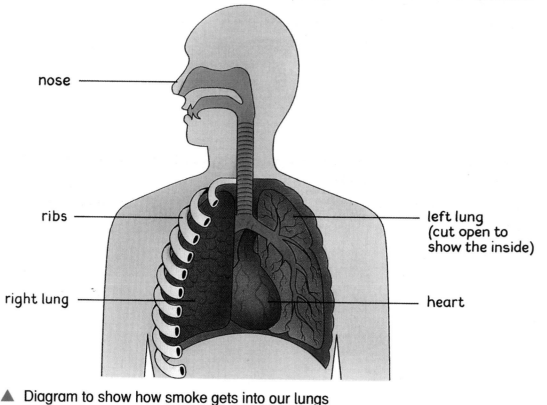

nose

ribs

right lung

left lung
(cut open to
show the inside)

heart

▲ Diagram to show how smoke gets into our lungs

A

1 What does pollution do to the air?

2 List **three** things that produce waste gases.

3 When you breathe in, where does the air end up?

4 Why is it better to breathe through your nose rather than to breathe through your mouth?

5 What might be harmed if you breathed too much polluted air into your body?

B

1 What does the diagram show you?

2 Look at the diagram. What other part of the body, apart from the lungs, do the ribs protect?

3 How can people help to stop air pollution?

4 What happens if one person smokes a cigarette in a room full of other people who never smoke cigarettes?

5 **a)** What does the photograph show you?
   b) Why do you think this particular photograph has been used?

C

Smoking is dangerous!

Using information from the opposite page make a **poster** that will be used to explain the dangers of smoking to children.

Use simple language so that the children will understand the message you are giving them.

Use pictures to help make the warnings clear.

The Wully-Wully

This is from a children's story about Babar the elephant's family, a rhinoceros, and another small creature.

Because Wully-Wully loved
the country so much
the children took him
on a picnic.
Rataxes the rhinoceros
watched them
from behind a bush.
'Oh ho,' he said to
himself,
'a Wully-Wully! If I can
catch him, he's mine!'
Poor little Wully-Wully
suspected
nothing. Nor did Pom
and Flora,
much less Alexander. With one bound Rataxes leapt
over the bush, sent the little elephants flying, and
caught Wully-Wully, who let out piercing cries.
But what could anyone do
against a fierce
rhinoceros?

A

1 Where is the Wully-Wully's favourite place?
2 What kind of animal does the Wully-Wully seem to be?
3 What are the names of the elephant children?
4 What is the name of the rhinoceros?
5 Why didn't the elephants see the rhinoceros?
6 How can you tell that Wully-Wully was afraid of the rhinoceros?

B

1 How did the rhinoceros get past the bush?
2 Why couldn't the elephants stop the rhinoceros?
3 What do you think the rhinoceros wanted to do to Wully-Wully?

C

Continue the story.
What will the elephant children do next?
What will happen to the rhinoceros?
What will happen to Wully-Wully?

Monsters

This is from a children's story by Russell Hoban that starts with ordinary events at home.

John was drawing a battle between an army of red monsters wielding hammers and an army of green monsters with tongs when his mother looked over his shoulder. "Don't you ever get tired of drawing monsters?" she said.

"Not really," said John. "Monsters are my favourite thing to draw."

"Still," said Mum, "there are so many other nice things to draw. There are houses and trees and birds and animals."

"Monsters are animals," said John.

"I mean real animals like dogs and cats," said Mum, "or even lions and tigers if you like."

"Monsters are real," said John.

"Have you ever seen one?" said Mum.

"I've seen them on TV," said John.

"Yes," said Mum, "but have you ever seen one walking around?"

"Not yet," said John. "Have you got any really big pieces of paper?"

"I've got some big sheets of brown wrapping paper," said Mum. She gave them to John.

"Thank you," said John. He took the wrapping paper and his felt-tip pens up to his room.

A

1 What does John like to draw most of all?

2 Only **one** of these sentences is true.
One army of monsters was coloured red and was carrying tongs.
One army of monsters was coloured green and was carrying hammers.
One army of monsters was coloured red and was carrying hammers.
Write down the sentence that is true.

3 Only **one** of these sentences is true.
John's mother wished that John would stop drawing pictures.
John's mother wished that John would draw a picture of something pleasant.
John's mother wished that John would draw even more pictures of monsters.
Write down the sentence that is true.

B

1 Why does John think monsters are real?

2 You want John to draw a picture of a monster for you.

First copy the table, and then fill in all the boxes, so that you can instruct him.

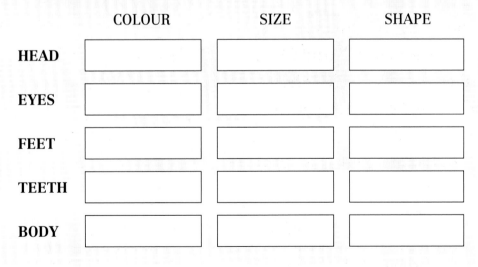

	COLOUR	SIZE	SHAPE
HEAD			
EYES			
FEET			
TEETH			
BODY			

C

Imagine that John drew the picture of the monster for you, put it in an envelope and sent it to you. As you opened the envelope the monster came alive! Write a story that tells what happened next. Start when the monster bursts out of the envelope.

The school skeleton

This is from a children's story by Sarah Garland where a lot of the action happens through the speech between characters.

After assembly, Mrs Suffolk passed me in the corridor.

"Come and help me, Clive. I've got a surprise for the class today."

"What is it?"

"A secret. Here. It's in this box."

Together we carried it to the classroom.

"It came in the post," said Mrs Suffolk, her eyes sparkling. "No note, nothing. It's an anonymous gift to the school."

The class crowded round. Mrs Suffolk lifted the lid and folded back the tissue paper.

There lay a pile of yellowed bones and, wrapped separately, a skull – a human skull!

"We're going to spend the whole morning putting it together," said Mrs Suffolk. "Here's some wire and a chart of a skeleton for us to copy. I'll show you how."

We each did separate bits. I did the backbones, which were fiddly but not as difficult as the hands and feet. Susan and Godfrey did them. We were all so absorbed and interested we didn't even stop at breaktime.

A

1 How did Clive's day at school begin?

2 What is the name of Clive's teacher?

3 Why do you think the box needed **two** people to carry it?

4 How did the box get to the school?

5 What were the children going to use the wire for?

6 How could the children tell the skeleton was a human skeleton?

7 How did the children know where to put the different bones?

B

1 Why do you think the skeleton was wrapped in tissue paper?

2 How can you tell that Mrs Suffolk knew making the skeleton would take a long time?

3 When she's telling Clive about the skeleton the teacher says, "No note, nothing." Then she says it is an **anonymous** gift. What do you think **anonymous** means?

4 How can you tell that the bones were very old bones?

5 Why do you think that the hands and feet were so difficult to fit together?

6 Why didn't the children want to go out at break?

C

When the children finish making the skeleton they leave it in the classroom. Next morning when they come into school they are amazed to discover a **letter** in the skeleton's hand!

The **letter** is as old and as yellow as the bones!

The teacher unfolds it carefully. It is covered in dust. As she reads it out the children gasp in amazement.

The **letter** tells them **who** the skeleton used to be, **why** it has been sent to the school and **who** sent the mystery gift.

Write the **letter** that was found in the skeleton's hand!

Stickers

This is a page from a catalogue published by Brainwaves, a company that sells stickers to schools.

FIRST CLASS STICKERS

1 Which animal appears on the sticker for being neat?

2 Why would you get a sticker with an elephant on it?

3 If you did a good painting, what would your sticker say?

MEMORY JOGGERS

4 What is on the sticker that reminds you to bring your swimming kit?

5 Which sticker would you like to be given?

6 Which sticker would you **not** like to be given?

HIGH FLYER AWARDS

7 How many stickers are there for school lunches?

8 Which sticker might you be given if you fell over in the playground?

9 What would your sticker say if you cleaned up the classroom?

1 Why do you think the Good Story sticker has a picture of a knight, a dragon and a castle on it?

2 Why do you think all the stickers have letters and numbers next to them?

3 a) Which sticker do you think has the best design?
 b) Why do you think this sticker is the best?

Design your own **sticker**.
It must have **words** and a **picture**.

Your sticker can be for:

Being kind
Being a good sport
Listening to instructions
Hard work
Making friends
Doing well in Science
Playing well in Music

Fire Orders

This is a notice pinned up to give people important information.

FIRE ORDERS

If you $\boxed{\text{see}}$ a fire leave the school quickly. Sound the fire alarm at one of the exits.

If you $\boxed{\text{hear}}$ the fire alarm:

1. Leave the building using the nearest staircase or exit door.
2. Do **not** stop to collect your things.
3. Do **not** run!
4. Close the classroom door.
5. Do not go back for **anything!**
6. Assemble with the rest of your class.
7. Wait quietly.
8. When your teacher calls your name, answer clearly.
9. Do not re-enter the building until you have been told it is safe to do so.
10. Do what your teacher tells you.

The assembly area for your class is:

> The Front Playground

STAY CALM!

A

1 Where might you find this notice?

2 Why do you think the notice has **red** letters and a **red** edge around it?

3 If you **see** a fire what should you do before you leave the building?

Now read the 10 orders very carefully.

B

1 If the fire alarm went off, where should the children in this class go?

2 Who will check to see if all the children are in the assembly area?

3 What do you think would happen if one of the children was missing?

4 Why do you think it is dangerous to run?

5 What might happen if you **did** go back for your pencil case?

6 Why do you think the children are told to wait **quietly**?

7 Who do you think would decide when it was safe to go back inside?

8 a) If you had to pick **one** of the orders as being the most important, which one would it be?

b) Why do you think this order is the most important?

C

Design a **notice** of your own.

Imagine there is a fast flowing river that rushes past your school. It is very dangerous. The sides are steep and muddy and the water is cold and deep.

Design a **notice** that will stop children from playing near the river.

Make sure your **notice** stands out so that everyone can see it.

You might like to use pictures as well as words.
You should use capital letters when you want the message to stand out.
You might like to use a numbered list of instructions.
Make sure your notice tells people what to do in a clear, simple way.

Ancient Greece

This is from a history information book about life in Greece over two thousand years ago.

Most Greek people lived in the country and were farmers. It was a hard life. The soil was rocky and did not grow very good crops. It rained too much in the winter and too little in the summer. The summer was also very hot. Grapes grew on the sides of the hills. Olives grew on trees on the poor soil, just as they do today. Their oil was used for cooking and for making lamps. On the better soil the Greeks grew corn. They used oxen to plough. They kept donkeys, sheep and goats.

This is what Greece looks like now. It has not changed much since the time of the Ancient Greeks. It is a hot, dry and rocky place.

A

1 What job was done by many of the Greeks who lived in the country?

2 Why was it difficult to plough some of the fields?

3 When was there never quite enough rain?

4 When was there far too much rain?

5 What crop did the Greeks grow in their best fields?

6 Name two other crops the Greeks grew.

7 What did the Greeks use to pull their ploughs?

B

1 In what sort of soil do olive trees grow?

2 After the olives were picked from the trees, what were they made into?

3 Why were the olives so useful to the Greeks?

4 How did the grapes and olives get ripe in the summer?

5 What is still the same in Greece today?

C

The writing on the opposite page gives us a lot of **information** about life in Ancient Greece. Use the **information** on the opposite page to fill in the gaps in the grid below.

Start by copying out the grid. When you have done that find the words in the passage that fit into the gaps.

Words that tell us about Ancient Greece:
1. Climate _ _ t
2. Jobs _ _ r _ e _ s
3. Crops _ o _ _ o _ _ _ _ _ _ _ _ p _ _
4. Animals _ x _ _ _ o _ _ _ _ _ _ _ _ t s _ _ _ _ e _

Places

This is from an information book that uses the geography of what places are like to explain the history of what happened long ago.

▶ Why do places begin?

Rivers

There may be a river where you live. Villages and towns often began near a river. The people could use the river water to drink and to cook with.

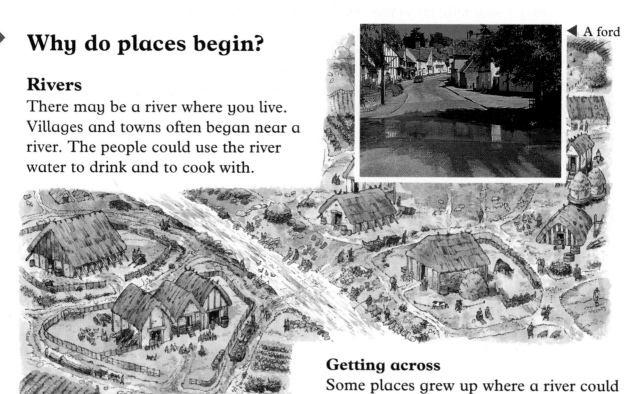

◀ A ford

▲ A village by a river long ago.

Getting across

Some places grew up where a river could be crossed. These places often have 'bridge' or 'ford' in their names. A ford is a place where a river is easy to cross.

6

1 Write down **two** things people used the river water for.

2 a) The drawing is of long ago, but the photo is modern.
How did the villagers in the drawing cross the river?

  b) Write down **one** thing that is the **same** in the photograph of the modern village and the drawing of the old village.

  c) Write down **two** things that are **different** in the photograph of the modern village and the drawing of the old village.

1 Describe the difference in the houses then and now.

2 Why don't towns and villages have to be near rivers nowadays?

3 A river runs through two villages.
One village is called **Bedford**, the other one is called **Bridgewater**.

  a) If the people get their feet wet when they cross the river do you think they live in **Bedford** or **Bridgewater**?

  b) Why do they get their feet wet?

Redraw the picture opposite as a **map**. This means that everything must look flat on the page, as if you were looking down from above.

Start by drawing the river. Write a **label** to show it is a river.

Draw the roads that run through the village. Write a **label** to show the **ford.**

Draw in the **fields** and **houses**. Write some **labels** to show they are fields and houses. (You might want to write what is in the different fields.)

When you have drawn in as much as you can, think of a **name** for the village. Make a large **label** so that everyone else knows its name.

The Beano

A complete comic strip story from *The Beano*.

A

1 Write down **two** ways the man treats the marrow like a baby.

2 Who guards the marrow before it goes to the show?

3 What surprises a lot of people when they go into the tent at the show?

4 What does the word **BADOOM!** describe?

5 Look carefully at the pictures and then write down a description of the clothes the person who brought the fake marrow to the show is wearing. Start from the top of his head and work your way down to his feet.

B

1 How has the cheat made his marrow so big?

2 Who does Les pretend to be?

3 Why does Les pretend to be this particular person?

4 What does Les do to prove that the owner of the giant marrow has cheated?

5 What is the real prize for the best vegetable?

6 At the very end Les makes a joke when he says, "That was a **marrow** escape". Write down the word that Les **should** have said. (Clue: It rhymes with marrow!)

C

Imagine you want to **re-tell** the story that appears in this comic strip to a person who cannot see the pictures.

1 When you write out your new version of the story you will have to describe what you can see.
At the beginning you might like to say something like this:
"When the squeaky old pram stopped the tall man lifted up a bundle. It wasn't a baby, it was a giant marrow!"

2 Imagine your story was read out on the radio. To make it more exciting you decide to add some **sound effects**. How could you make the following sounds?
The sound of the pram? The sounds made by the crowd of people at the show? The sound of the explosion? The sound of the bag hitting the man's head? Are there any other sounds you want to add?

Tintin

This is taken from a longer story about the well-known child detective.

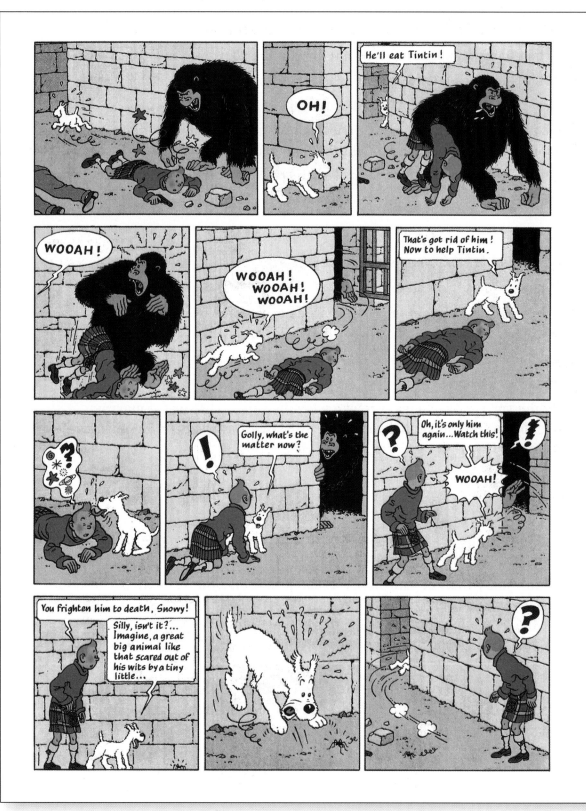

A

1 Why do you think the artist has drawn stars around Tintin's head?

2 What does the dog think the gorilla is going to do with Tintin?

3 What does the dog do that frightens the gorilla?

4 How does the dog help Tintin recover?

5 Why is Tintin frightened when he recovers?

6 How do you know this story happens in Scotland?

B

1 How do you know Tintin is surprised when the gorilla runs away?

2 Why is Tintin surprised when the dog runs away?

3 What frightens the dog?

4 How can you tell by looking at the **last** picture that it is the same place as the **first** picture?

5 What sort of story do you prefer?
   a) Stories like this that have only a few words but a great many pictures?
   b) Stories that have quite a lot of words and a few pictures?
   c) Stories that have a great many words and no pictures?

Why do you like to read stories like this?

C

Write what happens next, through using speech bubbles for each of these three characters.

Fairy Story

The verses in this short poem by Stevie Smith are only two lines long.
The two lines rhyme with each other.

Fairy Story

I went into the wood one day
And there I walked and lost my way

When it was so dark I could not see
A little creature came to me

He said if I would sing a song
The time would not be very long

But first I must let him hold my hand tight
Or else the wood would give me a fright

I sang a song, he let me go
But now I am home again there is nobody I know.

Stevie Smith

1 a) Where was the girl when she lost her way?
  b) Why had she gone there?

2 Why couldn't the girl see the creature very clearly?

3 What did the creature say the girl must do to make the time pass quickly?

4 What did the creature say would happen if she didn't hold his hand?

5 What did the creature do after the girl had finished singing?

Before you answer these questions read the last verse again.

1 Where did the girl go after she had sung her song?

2 What was different about this place?

3 What do you think had happened to the girl?

4 When the girl **first** met the creature, do you think she was pleased or sad to meet him? Explain why you think she was pleased or sad to meet him.

5 When the girl arrived home, do you think she was pleased or sad that she had met the little creature? Explain why you think she was pleased or sad.

This short poem tells a tale of mystery. It has a mysterious creature in a dark, mysterious wood.

Plan a mystery story of your own.

You might have a magical, mysterious creature living in a deep, dark cave or see a wizard at the door of a tall, windowless tower.

When you have planned what will happen in your story, turn it into a poem like the one on the opposite page.

Give each verse two lines and make both lines rhyme with each other.

Two poems

Both poems are about mystery creatures, and both are rhyming verses.

The Alien

The alien
Was as round as the moon.
Five legs he had
And his ears played a tune.
His hair was pink
And his knees were green,
He was the funniest thing I'd seen
As he danced in the door
Of his strange spacecraft,
He looked at me —
And laughed and laughed!

Julie Holder

The Mystery Creatures

They dwell on a planet not far
  from the Sun.
Some fly through the sky, while
  others just run.
Some have big heads which are
  hairless as tin,
while others have hair which
  sprouts from their skin.
They dig food from dirt, and
  gobble dead meat.

The young squeal like pigs if you
  tickle their feet.
They slurp, burp, and grunt;
  their manners are bad.
Their eyes become waterfalls
  When they feel sad.
Well, who are these creatures?
  Can you guess who?
The answer is easy: it's you,
  you, and YOU.

Wes Magee

A THE ALIEN

1 Write down **four** ways the Alien looks different to humans.

2 Write down **two** sounds the Alien makes.

3 Write down the word in the poem that **rhymes** with "craft".

4 Is this Alien real?

B THE MYSTERY CREATURES

1 Who are The Mystery Creatures?

2 What is the name of the place where they live?

3 Give an example of the food they dig from the earth.

4 Give an example of the dead meat they gobble up.

5 What are they doing when their eyes become waterfalls?

6 Write down the word in the poem that **rhymes** with "feet".

The wind and the sun

This is one of Aesop's fables, first told 2,500 years ago, and now written down in many versions.

The wind and the sun

One day the wind said to the sun, "Look at that man walking along the road. I can get his cloak off more quickly than you can."

"We will see about that," said the sun. "I will let you try first."

So the wind tried to make the man take off his cloak. He blew and blew, but the man only pulled his cloak more closely around himself.

44

45

"I have won," said the sun. "I made him take his cloak off."

Moral:
Kindness often gets things done more quickly than force.

"I give up," said the wind at last. "I cannot get his cloak off." Then the sun tried. He shone as hard as he could. The man soon became hot and took off his cloak.

46

47

A

1 The sun and the wind have a competition. Whose idea is it to have this competition?

2 What are the sun and the wind trying to make the man do?

3 How does the wind try to win the competition?

4 What does the man do when the wind tries to win?

5 How does the sun try to win the competition?

6 What does the man do when the sun tries to win the competition?

B

1 Did you prefer the wind or the sun in this story?

2 If the rain had entered the competition, would it have made the man take his cloak off?

3 If the competition had been to make the man put his cloak on, who do you think would have won?

4 If the competition had been to make the man take his hat off, who do you think would have won?

C

Stories like this that try to teach their readers a simple lesson are called **fables**. Fables usually have a **moral** at the end. The **moral** of this fable is that if you are kind to someone you often find that person will do something for you more quickly than if you were nasty to them.

Write a modern version of this **fable** that takes place in a school. In your story both Alex and Sita are trying to persuade Sam to clean out the class fish tank. Describe how Alex is nasty but Sita is kind to Sam.

Who persuades Sam in the end?

Morgiana and Ali Baba

This is the ending of a legend from Baghdad, told in words and pictures, about the servant Morgiana coming to the help of Ali Baba to kill the 40 thieves.

During the evening, a lamp went out. Morgiana took an oil pot and went to the courtyard to get some more. Her foot kicked a stone against the first jar.

"Is it time, master?" asked a voice. She realised there was a plot to harm Ali Baba and she went along the jars whispering, "Wait a while," in a gruff voice.

The last jar was full of oil. She filled her pot and re-lit the lamp. Morgiana put the pot on the fire and poured hot oil into each jar. That was the end of the robbers!

Once Ali Baba had gone to bed, the chief leaned out of a window and threw stones into the courtyard. This was the signal to attack, but nothing happened!

When he saw that his men were dead, he ran off into the night screaming. Ali Baba kept the secret of the treasure cave and gave half the fortune to Morgiana, having set her free. He spent the rest on bringing warmth and prosperity to the poor people of Baghdad.

This is the end of a very old story that was first told in Islamic countries hundreds of years ago. The story begins when Ali Baba sees the robber chief open the solid rock entrance to a cave.

The chief uses the magic words: *Open Sesame!*

The cave is where the robbers store all the treasure they have stolen. When the robbers have gone Ali Baba uses the magic words, goes into the cave and takes all the gold! The robbers, led by their chief, come to Ali Baba's house to steal the treasure back...

A

1 What time of day was it when Morgiana went into the courtyard?

2 What did Morgiana take with her into the courtyard?

3 What did Morgiana expect to find in the jars?

4 What did Morgiana find in the jars?

5 What did Morgiana use to kill the robbers?

B

1 Who did Morgiana work for?

2 Who was Morgiana trying to sound like when she whispered "Wait a while" in a gruff voice?

3 Morgiana was rewarded in **two** ways. What were they?

4 **a)** Do you think Ali Baba was a kind man or a cruel man?
   b) Write down a sentence from the story that shows how Ali Baba was either kind or cruel.

Imagine what the chief and his band of robbers must have felt like when they first found all the treasure gone! They must have been furious. They may have blamed each other. That was when they made the plan to come and hide in Ali Baba's house.

Write down the **conversation** the chief and the robbers had when they made their plan to get back the treasure. Start when the chief says the magic words: *Open Sesame!*

Art and the human body

This information book describes how artists have always made models, and drawn or painted pictures, of the human body.

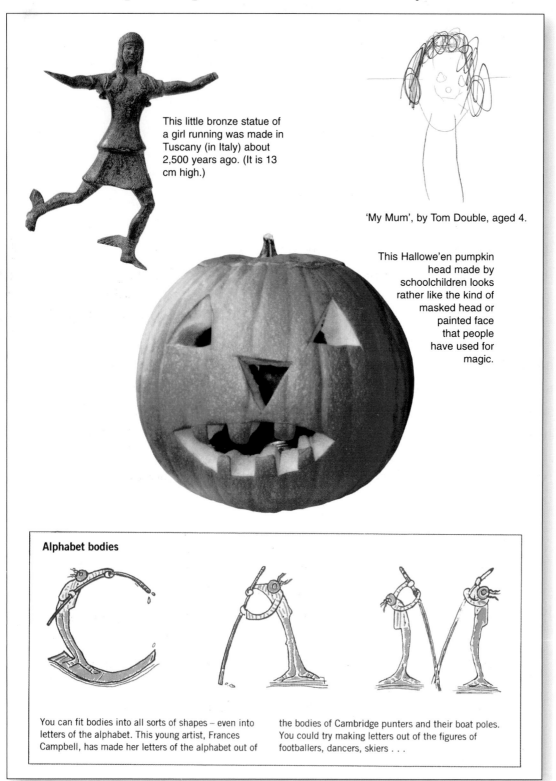

This little bronze statue of a girl running was made in Tuscany (in Italy) about 2,500 years ago. (It is 13 cm high.)

'My Mum', by Tom Double, aged 4.

This Hallowe'en pumpkin head made by schoolchildren looks rather like the kind of masked head or painted face that people have used for magic.

Alphabet bodies

You can fit bodies into all sorts of shapes – even into letters of the alphabet. This young artist, Frances Campbell, has made her letters of the alphabet out of the bodies of Cambridge punters and their boat poles. You could try making letters out of the figures of footballers, dancers, skiers . . .

A

1 What materials are the three objects made of?

  a)   **b)**   **c)**

2 When was each of them made?

  a)   **b)**   **c)**

3 How old do you think the artists were?

  a)   **b)**   **c)**

4 Which one of the objects do you like best, and why?

B

1 What are the three letters that Frances Campbell has drawn?

2 These three letters are just the start of a word. If you read the page carefully you should be able to work out the whole word. Write it down.

3 In the first letter Frances Campbell has not only used the person's body to make the letter's shape, she has also used **two** other things. What are they?

4 What tiny detail has Frances Campbell put into the first picture to show that the person is supposed to be on a boat floating down a river?

5 The opposite page comes from a book on Art. Here is a list of some of the chapters that are in the book. Choose the title of the chapter that you think this page comes from.

Face to Face   **What's Art For?**   **Telling a story**   **Body Language**

C

Frances Campbell used pictures of people to make her letters.

Try writing your name with pictures of things that you like.

If you are interested in sport you might make the letter **i** by using a cricket bat with a football on top.

If you are interested in animals you might make the letter **s** by drawing a snake.

If you are interested in reading you might make the letter **v** by drawing a half-open book.

Faces and masks

These two pages are from an information book on disguises.

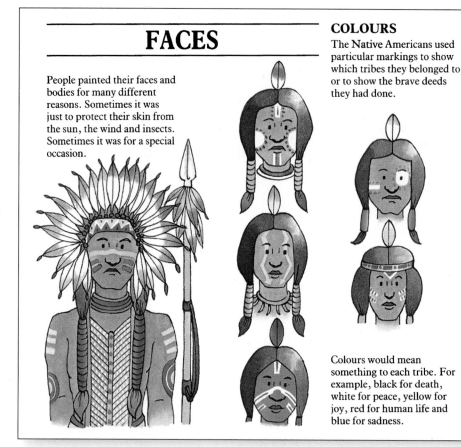

FACES

People painted their faces and bodies for many different reasons. Sometimes it was just to protect their skin from the sun, the wind and insects. Sometimes it was for a special occasion.

COLOURS

The Native Americans used particular markings to show which tribes they belonged to or to show the brave deeds they had done.

Colours would mean something to each tribe. For example, black for death, white for peace, yellow for joy, red for human life and blue for sadness.

A FACES

1 How did these people protect their skin?

2 Write down **three** things people needed to protect their skin from.

3 Give **another** reason why people painted their skin.

4 Give **two** reasons why Native Americans used to paint their faces.

5 a) If you met a Native American who was wearing **white** paint, would you be scared or would you be happy?

b) What would you feel if they were wearing **blue** paint?

B

Imagine you are a Native American.

Draw a picture of your face. Invent a colourful design that shows how you feel. Underneath the picture explain why you have chosen these colours and shapes.

MASKS

Masks were very important too as they could frighten, amuse or impress other people.

These are different kinds of masks that are worn in different parts of the world today.

Japanese Theatre

Circus

Caribbean Carnival

MASKS

1 a) Which one of the masks in the pictures is meant to **frighten** people?
  b) How does it frighten people?

2 a) Which one of the masks in the pictures is meant to **amuse** people?
  b) Which part of this mask would make you laugh?

3 a) Which one of the masks in the pictures is meant to **impress** people?
  b) Why would this mask be difficult to make?

4 a) Which mask is your favourite?
  b) Why do like this mask?

Design a mask of your own, to make you look **sad**.

Write underneath your design what you have done to make it look like the face of someone who is **sad**.

Life in an Indian village

This page from an information book gives you a description of Indian village life solely through pictures.

The village day

The pictures show a day in the life of two children, Lakshmi and her brother Ramu, their mother Kamala and their father Gopal.

1 In every picture the artist has drawn the family's house. How has the artist shown what time of day it is?

2 What jobs do the children do while Kamala is preparing their breakfast?

3 What does Gopal do while his children are walking to school?

4 While the children are at school Kamala is hard at work. What does she do while her children are at school?

5 How can you tell the family has no electricity in their house?

6 What can we tell from the pictures about bed time in an Indian village?

7 How is cooking in an Indian village different to cooking in your house?

1 a) Who do you think has the busiest day?
   b) List **three** tasks this person does during the day.

2 a) Which member of the family would you like to be?
   b) Which part of their day would you like best?
   c) Explain why you chose this part of the day.

3 If you went from where you live now to live in an Indian village, what would you miss most of all? Give your reasons.

Imagine you are either Lakshmi or Ramu. Using the pictures to help you write down an entry from your **diary**. It should be about a single day in your life in the village. Don't just put down all the things you **do**, make sure you write down how you **feel** about doing these things as well.

You might be happy because you have time to read.

You might be cross because you don't have a television!

You might be pleased that the weather is warm, even at night.

You might be sad because your mother has to work so hard.

You might complain you have to do a job that others don't have to do.

How to make a flick book

These are instructions from a set of worksheets on how films are made.

■ **What you need;**

Pencil   Note pad   Colouring pens

■ **What to do;**

1. Simply copy or trace these drawings onto the bottom right hand corner of your pad.

2. Start with drawing number 1 and draw it on the last page of your pad.

3. Now draw number 2 on the next to last page and so on.

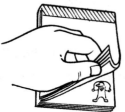

4. When you have drawn all 10 pictures, flick the corners of the pad and watch the pictures come alive!

A

1 What will the pictures show when you flick through them?

2 When you are making a flick book where do you draw your first picture?

3 Where exactly on the page of the pad do the pictures have to be drawn?

4 a) What do you notice about the eyes of the flick book character?
   b) What do you notice about the mouth of the flick book character?

5 What else changes through the ten pictures?

B

1 What is the connection between these moving pictures and how a cartoon film is made?

2 How does it help you to understand about cartoon films?

C

The worksheet contains **instructions**.
To begin with the worksheet tells you what you **need**.
Then it lists the **four** things you must **do**.
The **pictures** help you understand how to follow the instructions.

Using the same method write some **instructions** of your own.

Imagine you have to explain to some aliens how things are done on Earth.

1 Write a set of **four instructions** telling the aliens how to sharpen a pencil.

2 Write a set of **four instructions** telling the aliens how to get ready for school.

3 Write a set of **four instructions** telling the aliens how to play your favourite game.

Sources

The texts used in this book are extracted from the following full sources, and we are grateful for their permission to reproduce copyright material.

p 4   From *The Oxford Children's Pocket Book of Living Things* by S Goodman (OUP, 1995), reproduced by permission of Oxford University Press.

p 6   From *The Wind in the Willows* Collection No 5 (29.1.97), reproduced by permission of Marvel Comics, a division of Panini UK Ltd.

p 8   Text and illustrations by Ian Beck for 'Incey Wincey Spider' from *Oxford Nursery Book* (OUP, 1995), reproduced by permission of The Agency (London) Ltd, © Ian Beck 1995. All rights reserved and enquiries to The Agency (London) Ltd, 24 Pottery Lane, London W11 4LZ fax: 0171 727 9037

p 10   From *The Nursery Companion* by Iona and Peter Opie (OUP, 1980), reproduced by permission of Oxford University Press.

p 12   From *Fred* by Posy Simmonds (Cape, 1987), reproduced by permission of Random House (UK) Ltd.

p 14   From *Billy and Belle* by Sarah Garland (Reinhardt, 1992), reproduced by permission of Reinhardt Books.

p 16   From *How to Look After Your Rabbit* by Colin and Jacqui Hawkins, © 1995 Colin and Jacqui Hawkins, reproduced by permission of the publisher Walker Books Ltd.

p 18   From *Protecting Our Wildlife* by Terry Jennings (OUP Factfinders, 1995) reproduced by permission of Oxford University Press.
Photographs by Michael Leach reproduced by permission of Michael Leach and Oxford Scientific Films.

p 22   From *Outside Now – May and June* by Linton & Terry (Bell & Hyman, 1985) reproduced by permission of HarperCollins Publishers Ltd.

p 24   Extract from *Watching Books – Cats* adapted from the Dutch text of Frans Hoppenbrouwers, illustrated by Diet van Beek (Ginn, 1980), © L C G Malmberg B V.

p 26   From *Incredible Skeleton Secrets* by Angela Wilkes (Dorling Kindersley, 1994), reproduced by permission of the publishers.

p 28   From *Pollution* by Terry Jennings (OUP Factfinders, 1995), reproduced by permission of Oxford University Press.
Photograph by John Leighton reproduced by permission of Network Photographers Ltd.

p 30   From *Babar and the Wully-Wully* by Jean de Brunhoff (Methuen Children's Books, 1977), Copyright © Lauren de Brunhoff 1977, translation Copyright © Methuen Children's Books 1977, reproduced by permission of Reed Consumer Books Ltd.

p 32   Text from *Monsters* by Russell Hoban (Gollancz, 1989) reproduced by permission of David Higham Associates.
Illustration by Quentin Blake, reproduced by permission of A P Watt Ltd on behalf of Quentin Blake.

p 34   Text and illustration from *Clive and the Missing Finger* by Sarah Garland (A & C Black [Publishers] Ltd, 1994), reproduced by permission of the publishers.

p 36   Stickers from *Brainwaves Spring Catalogue* 1997, reproduced by permission of Brainwaves Stickers, Trewithan Parc, Lostwithiel, Cornwall PL22 0BD. Tel 01208 873096/ Fax 01208 873872

p 40   From *The Ancient Greeks* by Pat Taylor, Copyright © Pat Taylor 1991 (*Ancient Civilizations* by Pat Taylor and Jane Shuter, Heinemann Educational Books), reproduced by permission of Heinemann Educational, a division of Reed Educational and Professional Publishing Ltd.

p 42   From *Exploring Where You Live* by Terry Jennings (OUP Factfinders, 1995) reproduced by permission of Oxford University Press.
Photograph of Kersey, Suffolk reproduced by permission of Images Colour Library Limited.

p 44   'Les Pretend' page from *The Beano*, Copyright © D C Thomson & Co Ltd 1996, reproduced by permission of D C Thomson & Co Ltd.

p 46   Text extract in English translation from *Tintin: The Black Island* by Herge (Methuen Children's Books, 1990), Text Copyright © 1966 Methuen & Co Ltd, reproduced by permission of Reed Consumer Books Ltd.
Illustrations Copyright © 1956, 1984 by Casterman, reproduced by permission of Moulinsart SA, Brussels.

p 48   'Fairy Story' by Stevie Smith from *The Collected Poems* of *Stevie Smith* (Penguin 20th Century Classics), Copyright ©1972 by Stevie Smith, reproduced by permission of James MacGibbon.
Illustrated page reproduced from *The Oxford Book of Story Poems* by Michael Harrison and Christopher Stuart-Clark (OUP, 1990) by permission of Oxford University Press.

p 50   'The Alien' by Julie Holder reprinted by permission of the author, and 'The Mystery Creatures' by Wes Magee reprinted by permission of the author, both first published in John Foster (ed): *A Third Poetry Book* (OUP, 1982).
Illustrated page reproduced by permission of Oxford University Press.

p 52   Text and illustration for 'The wind and the sun' from *A First Book of Aesop's Fables* (1974) by Marie Stuart, reproduced by permission of Ladybird Books Limited.

p 54   From 'Ali Baba and the Forty Thieves' from *I Love to Read Fairy Tales*, Issue 19, Copyright © The Redan Company, 1996, reproduced by permission of The Redan Company Limited.

p 56   Material from *What is Art?* by Rosemary Davidson (OUP, 1993), used by permission of Cynthia Parzych Publishing, Inc.
Photograph of Pumpkin by Rosemary Davidson, drawing 'My Mum' by Tom Double, Frances Campbell print [alphabet] from the collection of Mr and Mrs John A A Turner, all reproduced by permission of Cynthia Parzych Publishing, Inc.

p 58   From *Disguises* by Joan Weston, (Octopus [Wiz Pax] 1988), Copyright © Octopus Publishing Group Ltd 1988, reproduced by permission of Reed Consumer Books Ltd.

p 60   Material from *India* by Natasha Talyarkhan (Macdonald, 1975) reproduced by permission of Wayland Publishers.

p 62   Page from UCI Schools Resource Pack 1996, reproduced by permission of United Cinemas International (UK) Ltd.

Although we have tried to trace and contact all copyright holders before publication this has not always been possible. If notified we will be pleased to rectify any errors or omissions at the earliest opportunity.